IMAGES
of America

CHESAPEAKE BAY
DEADRISE BOATS

This classic round-stern deadrise bateau was owned by Will Shackelford of Urbanna, Virginia. This photograph was taken in 1959 on the Rappahannock River. Shackelford used the boat to trotline for hard crabs and hand tong for oysters. This is an early classic bateau showing an engine and engine box located near the stern and no house/pilothouse. The evolution of deadrise construction on Chesapeake Bay was greatly enhanced by the introduction of internal combustion engines in the 1880s. Early two- and four-cycle engines in small deadrise boats were better than a sculling paddle in that "they would go all day" but, in some cases, only moved the boat a bit faster than a good sculler. (Courtesy of Carroll C. Chowning Jr.)

ON THE COVER: The *Ellen Marie* was built in 1926 in Susan, Virginia, by L.R. Smith and Alton Smith. This photograph shows a unique time in the history of deadrise boats when workboats were lightened down to go racing. No matter the generation, deadrise boat owners took pride in having the fastest boat. This photograph was taken on a race day. The pilothouse and extra weight were pulled off for speed. Race day was an exciting day when family and friends were aboard to be a part of the festivities. The *Ellen Marie* died in 2021 in Gloucester County, Virginia, just one county over from where she was built. Her hull snapped in two when the boat was being hauled out of the water. (Courtesy of the *Gloucester-Mathews Gazette-Journal*.)

IMAGES
of America

CHESAPEAKE BAY
DEADRISE BOATS

Larry S. Chowning

ARCADIA
PUBLISHING

Published by Arcadia Publishing
Charleston, South Carolina

Printed in the United States of America

Library of Congress Control Number: 2023950808

For all general information, please contact Arcadia Publishing:
Telephone 843-853-2070
Fax 843-853-0044
E-mail sales@arcadiapublishing.com
For customer service and orders:
Toll-Free 1-888-313-2665

Visit us on the Internet at www.arcadiapublishing.com

Dedicated to my father, H.S. Chowning Jr., and my great uncle Charles Henry Palmer Jr., who both inspired me to look at life a little different

CONTENTS

ACKNOWLEDGMENTS

For the past 40 years, I have written about and photographed wooden Chesapeake Bay deadrise boats. My love of the boats and the culture that surrounds it goes back to my childhood.

Around 1956, my father, Henry Shepherd "Shep" Chowning Jr., purchased a wooden deadrise that he named *Miss Susan* after my sister. Although we had long since sold the boat when my mother died in 2021, I came across the worn and tattered "Certificate of Award of Number to a Documented Vessel" for the *Miss Susan* inside a dresser draw.

The boat was built in Mathews County, Virginia, in 1952 by Edgar L. Diggs and Son in Peary, Virginia. She was twenty-five feet, four inches long by seven feet, six inches wide by two feet draft. She was powered by a 100-horsepower flathead Gray Marine inboard engine. We had always heard she had been built as an oyster watch boat and was manned at night near oyster beds to discourage thievery.

It was from the decks of this boat at a young age that I developed a curiosity, excitement, and love of the Bay and its tributaries. I also learned how to operate a boat. *Miss Susan* was used regularly by my family on weekends in the spring and summer for bottom fishing and in the Fall and winter to troll for rockfish. At an early age, Dad would let me take the helm and guide the boat home into Urbanna Creek. It was on the *Miss Susan* at the age of 12 that I earned my Boy Scout boating merit badge. I took her out from the family boathouse and brought her home without a hitch. My scoutmaster Billy VanWagen who was the only one besides myself aboard simply said, "You can certainly drive a boat."

I thank my father for introducing me at a young age to the Chesapeake Bay deadrise boats and encouraging me to go out on the water. My writings on the bay have in part been because of his love of boats and the water. By sharing it with me, it has truly enriched my life.

INTRODUCTION

The deadrise/cross-planked boatbuilding style started on Chesapeake Bay in the 1880s as wooden boatbuilders began to shift away from building boats out of logs to building planked V-bottom, hard chine boats.

Maritime historian Howard I. Chapelle said in his writings that there were early experiments with deadrise and cross-planked boats in New England and the Deep South on the Gulf of Mexico, but the style did not become popular there.

The choppy water conditions of Chesapeake Bay were ideal for a shoal draft, V-bottom style of boat. This along with the availability of wooden planks; a dynamic backyard boatbuilding industry; and diverse inshore fisheries that supported a bay-wide fleet and encouraged the development of various sizes and styles of boats all contributed to the wooden deadrise and cross-planked movement on the bay.

For nearly a century and a half, bay watermen and others have revered the style of boat which led Maryland's legislature in 1985 to name the deadrise and cross-planked sailing skipjack the state boat of Maryland and in 1988 Virginia legislature named the classic wooden deadrise Virginia's state boat.

The culture of deadrise and cross-planked boat building grew from a much broader wood culture that for generations had relied on wood. Whether you lived in Tidewater Virginia or Maryland or other regions across this nation, wood was a primary material used to sustain day-to-day life. Virginia and Maryland woodworkers used wood in every aspect of life—from building homes, furniture, hog troughs, forks and spoons, decoys, coffins, horse-drawn carriages, wooden fishnet needles, gristmill gears, and boats.

Over time, an understanding of the best wood for a particular job, the best tools for shaping a hull, and the best fasteners for attaching wood all evolved so that boatbuilders were able to perfect and polish their craft.

The business of building wooden boats covered a broad pool of talented boatbuilders ranging from one end of the Chesapeake Bay to the other end. Even though bay maritime historians can point to specific areas of the bay region that excelled in building wooden boats, it was a bay-wide cottage industry. When boats were the main means of transportation, almost every Tidewater city, town, village, and neighborhood on the water had someone skilled in repairing and building wooden boats.

The modern Chesapeake Bay wooden V-bottom deadrise workboat was the grand finale of a boatbuilding experiment that spanned centuries. Even though, most maritime historians trace the beginning of V-bottom deadrise boats on the bay to the 1880s, its roots on Chesapeake Bay and in America go back much further.

The early Chesapeake Bay boats were built out of logs and even to this day elements of log canoe construction are found in planked-built deadrise boats. Early log canoe builders formed the V-shape in the bow and stern using a "chunk" system of layering blocks of wood and then shaving them down in the bow and stern to a V-shape. The same V-shape style can be found in modern deadrise wooden boats, made out of staving wood (short, narrow planks) rather than blocks of wood. Interestingly, the chunk system was used by early deadrise and cross-planked boatbuilders to shape round or elliptical sterns on boats. Early builders also experimented with chunk bows. Blocks of wood used to shape a V-bow were called head blocks and the construction method was referred to as building a "chunk bow" or "chunk forefoot." When used in the stern, it was referred to as a "chunk stern."

Before the term "deadrise" was used to identify the style on the Chesapeake, planked, hard-chine boats were referred to as bateaux (the French word for boats). Early-20th-century flat-bottom tonging and pound-net skiffs, along with V-bottom boats in those fisheries, were often referred to as bateaux. Some pound-net fishermen abbreviated the name "bateaux" and used the name "bats," and some referred to small flat-bottom and V-bottom boats as "towbats." These were boats towed behind the larger boats and used in working fish nets.

The term "deadrise" is a relatively modern term for wooden V-bottom, hard chine boats. The late Joe Gregory wrote a book entitled *Deadrise is from here –To Yonder*, which is the common answer that is given by a bay boatbuilder standing beside his nearly completed boat with a stick in hand pointing to the V-shape in the bottom. The technical answer for deadrise is the "dead" referring to the straight rise of the wood from the keel rabbet to the chine. This usually includes all bottom planking from the bow staving to near the stern.

Over time, the use of the word "deadrise" became more associated with the entire boat than just the V-planking at the bottom. That is why today people refer to the V-bottom and cross-planked boat, in a general way, as the Chesapeake Bay Deadrise.

The origin of the use of the term deadrise has prompted debate. Most Bay maritime historians and boatbuilders believe that the deadrise term originated with the V-bottom and hard chine. However, there are some creditable boatbuilders who believe that the term "deadwood" is where the name deadrise originated. Virginia boatbuilders use the name deadwood for the wood that is cut and thrown away when shaping the bottom of a boat. Paula J. Johnson said in her book *The Workboats of Smith Island* that Smith Island, Maryland, boatbuilders refer to deadwood as the thick craved planking in the fore-foot of a V-bottom boat, which is referred to in Virginia as staving wood.

Although some may differ in their belief as to the origin of the term deadrise, they all agree that the development of the wooden deadrise boat was a game changer in the maritime life and history of Chesapeake Bay. The V-bottom/cross-planked style has been built out of wood, fiberglass, and aluminum, and to date, no one has found a more efficient style of boat for the bay than the V-bottom deadrise.

One

DIVERSITY

Over the generations, the Chesapeake Bay deadrise hull has been used for many types of commercial work and recreational play. The size of the boats ranged from 12-foot skiffs to the largest one ever built, the 97-foot-long *MaryDel*. The boats carried generations of families on their annual summertime blackberry picking adventures; hauled Pasha, a 2,775-pound elephant to a circus on Tangier Island; delivered milk daily from the local dairy across the creek; carried grocery stock to bay islands; bused high school children from Smith Island, Maryland, to Crisfield High School and students from Fleeton, Virginia, to schools in Reedville; hauled ice to the Town of Urbanna from the block ice plant across the river in Irvington; and carried everything that Methodist preacher owned from Norfolk to Onancock when he received his transfer papers. Large V-bottom boats hauled freight from one end of the bay to the other. The deadrise platform also worked well in the many different bay fisheries. Oyster, crab, and conch dredges; oyster and clam patent tongs; hand oyster tongs; crab, peeler, fish, eel, and conch pots; crab nets, trotlines, crab scrapes, and peeler pounds; hydraulic clam escalator dredges; and haul seines, pound nets, and gill-nets were worked from deadrise boats. The hull style was great for work or pleasure. Many Tidewater Virginia and Maryland folk owned deadrise yachts or converted workboats used exclusively for pleasure. The boats provided lifelong memories of lazy summer days bottom fishing with family members, laid-back moments watching the annual Labor Day boat races, and the sweet recollection of the taste of grandma's fried chicken on the family picnic/fishing trip out on the boat.

Wooden boats were built for all ages, and although this is not a deadrise, it was built with love for those Eastern Shore children. The cross-planked, flat-bottom skiff was the forerunner of the deadrise hull, and for most boys and girls, their boating experiences began with a flat-bottom skiff. (Courtesy of Andy Teeling.)

This photograph was taken at Lennie and Alton Smiths' boatyard on Pepper Creek in Mathews County, Virginia, in the 1930s. Men are taking a lunch break before going back to work. The Smith family were generational Mathews County boatbuilders, and over time, the family spread to Gloucester and York Counties and built wooden deadrise boats there. (Courtesy of the *Gloucester-Mathews Gazette-Journal*.)

The Chesapeake deadrise is often associated with workboats, but many were built solely for pleasure and transportation. The deadrise hull was originally designed for sail, as this photograph reflects, but as internal combustion engines arrived on the scene, boatbuilders made adjustments in hulls to accommodate engines. (Courtesy of the Dr. A.L. VanName Jr. Collection, Deltaville Maritime Museum.)

When internal combustion engines were introduced into bay boats logged hull sailboats were converted to power and some canoe builders began building log boats for power. As planked deadrise boats became more popular and good logs scarce, log boat construction declined, and deadrise and cross-planked construction became the next step in the evolution of wooden boatbuilding on the Chesapeake. (Courtesy of Deltaville Maritime Museum.)

The boat in the foreground is a deadrise sailboat named *Valkirie* and built for pleasure. The *Union*, a deadrise-style fishing party boat, is up against the *Valkirie*. The boat at the end of the dock is the buyboat *Helen Windsor*, originally a sail-powered bugeye built in 1900 by B.P. Miles of Oriole, Maryland. She has a round-bilge hull and is not a deadrise hull. (Courtesy of Buddy Wyker.)

The deadrise fishing party boat *Union* has a "wireless mast" atop her house. The mast was installed so copper wiring could be attached to allow the skipper to broadcast by way of Morse code. Owner Jack Wyker installed the mast but did not get around to installing the wiring. (Courtesy of Buddy Wyker.)

This 1940s photograph shows deadrise workboats moored to stakes in the background. When a boat owner went to use his boat, he paddled out in a skiff, tied the skiff to the stake to mark his stake spot, and after a ride in the big boat, the skiff provided transportation back to shore. (Courtesy of Wanda Greenwood Hollberg.)

This photograph of the *Renell K* was taken in 1964. The boat was owned by waterman Harold Kennard of Deltaville, Virginia. There is a house for storage and no pilothouse. *Renell K* was used in the spring and summer crab pot fishery and in the Fall and winter hand tong oyster fishery. (Courtesy of Joe Conboy.)

When this photograph was taken at C.H. Rice and Son Boatyard in Fairport, Virginia, the menhaden steamer *Hiawatha* with its two purse boats alongside was likely the main focus of the photographer. The two deadrise boats near the bow of the steamer and the one in the left corner, however, speak to the diversity of house/pilothouse styles used on deadrise hulls. (Courtesy of Ed Rice.)

Small railways were scattered on creeks and coves throughout the Chesapeake Bay region. The very existence of the bay's deadrise fleet depended on railways. This photograph was taken of Morton Clarke's Railway at Regent, Virginia, in the early 1990s. The building on the left had been used as a corn crib, and the one on the right, a chicken house on a nearby farm before being moved and becoming part of the railway. (Author's collection.)

The primitive house on this deadrise is adorned with family and neighborhood children. A man's deadrise boat played an important part in the lives of Tidewater Virginia and Maryland families. For many, it provided a platform for sustenance and to earn monetary means to support the family. The tarpaper roof covering the house was an inexpensive way of protecting the roof. (Courtesy of Emily Chowning.)

When internal combustion engines were introduced into bay boats, the first inclination was to convert sail-powered log boats to power boats. Sail- and wind-driven log boats had for centuries been the main platform for bay mariners. This motor-powered log boat marked the final evolution of log boat construction as deadrise and cross-planked styles became the next step in the evolution of wooden boatbuilding on the Chesapeake. (Author's collection.)

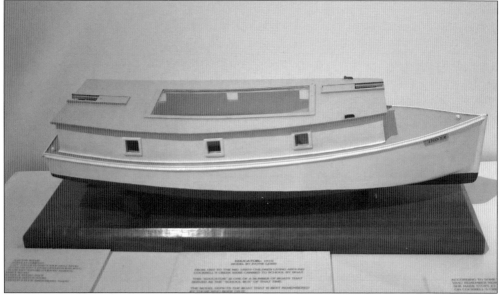

This boat model is of a deadrise boat named *Educator*. From 1907 to the mid-1920s, school-age children living on Cockrell Creek near Reedville, Fleeton, and Fairport, Virginia, were carried to school by boat. This model style is one of a number of boats that served as the school bus and another example of the diversity of use of the bay's wooden deadrise boats. The model was made by Payne Lewis. (Courtesy of the Reedville Fishermen's Museum.)

Floran was a deadrise yacht built by George P. Butler of Reedville, Virginia. Butler's son George M. Butler lives today on four acres of land on Cockrell Creek. Reed Randolph had Butler's father build the *Floran* in the 1940s and paid for a portion of the boat with those four acres. Wooden deadrise yachts were popular in the 1940s, 1950s, and 1960s. (Courtesy of Carroll C. Chowning Jr.)

These Virginia-built boats were used in the state's charter boat and oyster fisheries and owned and operated by African American captains on Locklies Creek in Topping, Virginia. Ownership of a vessel was a sign of prosperity, and the river provided year-round work. Black watermen could rely on the river in bad and good times, and a good deadrise boat was the platform that made it happen. (Author's collection.)

The *Kristen Marie*, *Lisa Marie*, and another boat from Poquoson, Virginia, are rafted off together here, preparing to participate in workboat races on the York River. The *Lisa Marie* is decorated to the hilt with flags on her rigging. Watermen enjoy such events to show off their boats. They take pride in who built their boats, how they look, and how fast they go. (Author's collection.)

Maria Lynn, *Restless*, and *Rainbow Chaser* are up on plane in a workboat race on York River. Whether under sail or power, boat owners take pride in owning a fast boat and look forward to annual workboat races to prove that their boat is "faster than your boat." The winner of the race had bragging rights until the next race was lost. (Author's collection.)

The *Mary Joan* was used as a patent tong clam rig in the Chesapeake Bay and owned by the legendary clammer Wilbur Denvy "Dink" Miller. Dink was a colorful man who won the *Mary Joan* in a poker game when he was working on an oyster "drudge" boat in York River. "When the boys got into a game one cold night, Dink came away with the boat," said Gloucester County, Virginia, clammer Fred Setterholm, who was there. (Author's collection.)

This photograph, taken on Smith Island, Maryland, in the 1980s, shows the size range of deadrise boats. The 65-foot *Estelle Leonard* was built in 1927 by Jabez Tyler of Cambridge, Maryland. *Miss Violet* is a classic 42-foot deadrise workboat, and the deck boat between the two is 55 feet long. The deadrise in the distance and tied to a dock is a classic Tangier Island Barcat. (Author's collection.)

Lord Mott Corporation of Baltimore, Maryland, established Lord Mott Canning Factory in Urbanna, Virginia, in the 1930s. The plant canned vegetables and tomatoes and utilized large deadrise boats to haul products, cans, and ingredients. This photograph taken in 1959 shows the plant built out on the water and the unique double-decker boat the *Big Muriel Eileen*, a 85-foot deadrise freighter owned by the corporation. (Courtesy of Carroll C. Chowning Jr.)

This Hoopers Island draketail, or ducktail or dovetail, as called by some, originated from the Hoopers Island, Maryland, area. These boats were modeled after early racing launches and torpedo boats. Many of the early draketails were easily driven up to 10 knots, with the five- to fifteen-horsepower engines available. The boats sported a rounded, fantail stern with a reverse rake and chine that followed the waterline throughout the length of the boat. (Courtesy of Ben Williams.)

This draketail deck boat was up on the rails at Winegar's Marine Railway in Lancaster County, Virginia, in the 1940s. The draketail style was adapted to large Chesapeake Bay buyboats but was unique and rare. Irving F. and Walter B. Cannon were two well-known builders who constructed classic draketail deck boats on Fishing Creek on Hoopers Island. (Courtesy of Cathy Davenport.)

This 42-foot deadrise has a 12-by-12-inch fir keel that is set in place with the aid of two block and tackles extended from the ceiling of the boat shop. The hardest part of building a deadrise is setting it up at the beginning of construction. This boat is being built in Bohannon, Virginia, by boatbuilder Bill Keeling. This is a rare sight today on Chesapeake Bay. (Author's collection.)

This photograph shows the startup of a 42-foot deadrise boat setup upside down and looking at a solid-piece horn timber and shaft log. The introduction of solid-piece horn timbers in the 1940s greatly improved the longevity of deadrise boats. Prior to then horn timbers were pieced and bolted together, sometimes in as many as seven pieces and these joints were highly susceptible to rot and leakage. The horn timber ties the keel and transom together and creates a concave shape to the stern. (Author's collection.)

This round-stern deadrise has a rubber tire fender tied to the stern to protect it from bumping up against a dock or keeping another boat from hitting up against the stern. Watermen have been innovative over the years in creating ways to protect, maintain, and work their boats. The ordinary automobile tire was used by many watermen as stern and side fenders. (Courtesy of Joe Conboy.)

Rope bow fenders were used to protect the bows and sides of bay boats. This rope fender is being used on a flat-bottom fiberglass towbat skiff being used in the Virginia pound-net fishery. Rope bow fenders were used on all types and sizes of bay boats and a good fender maker was a treasured craftsman up and down the bay. (Author's collection.)

The diversity of bay deadrise boats can be seen in the size and in the names of the boats. The name *Little Fat Buddy* speaks to the boat having a short and stout appearance. The size of deadrise boats was often determined by the fishery the boat was working or the distance the boat traveled to and from fishing grounds. (Author's collection.)

This photograph was taken at A.C. Fisher Jr. Marine Railway in Wicomico Church, Virginia, and further speaks to the diversity of the types of names used around the bay on deadrise boats. *Home Brew* is getting a fresh spring coat of paint at the railway, and a name painter was brought in to freshen up the name and add a pair of beer bottles. (Author's collection.)

The diversity of the boats was also tied to materials used to build boats. Naturally, wood was the primary material but in the early 1970s pioneers in the use of fiberglass boatbuilding came on the bay scene. One of those early pioneers was Bill and Bob Lippinscott Jr., owners of Chesapeake Marine Industries Inc. of Trappe, Maryland. This was one of their early fiberglass deadrise boats. (Courtesy of Chesapeake Marine Industries Inc.)

One of the most unique builders on the bay is Eric Hedberg of Mathews County, Virginia, who uses PVC sheets and planks to build his boats. Hedberg said that a boat built out of PVC "looks like a wood boat, acts like a wood boat and feels like a wood boat," but does not have maintenance issues that go along with a wood boat. (Author's collection.)

This photograph shows a man attaching a rudder to a deadrise at Reedville Marine Railway in Reedville, Virginia, sometime in the 1940s. When internal combustion engines took the place of mast and sail for power on boats, one of the most difficult elements of the transition was figuring out the best way to install the prop and rudder. Some configurations were awkward as this photograph reflects. (Courtesy of Becky and George Butler.)

Two

FINFISH BOATS

When the deadrise hull was introduced to the bay, organized recreation and commercial finfish fishing were well established. As the population grew along the bay and lifestyles changed, particularly after World War II, there was more free time for recreation. The wooden deadrise hull was the main choice for many pleasure boaters.

That era after World War II found city folk longing for the country and shores of Chesapeake Bay. Some had visited during steamboat days while others grew up or had family in Tidewater Virginia and Maryland. Going fishing lured summer folks to the river and bay. The bay's charter boat fishery "For Hire" provided a day out on the water to wet a fishing line.

As demand for commercial fishing grew, there was also an increased demand for larger and more refined deadrise boats. Haul seine gear was introduced to the Chesapeake by early English settlers who settled in Maryland and Virginia and is still being used today on the Chesapeake. Larger boats were required in this fishery when in 1938 Earl Hudgins of Mathews County, Virginia, invented the purse pocket on the haul seine. A purse pocket closes and secures the catch allowing fishermen to detach the pocket from the net to haul out into deeper water. There, the fish were more efficiently removed from the net and loaded into the boat. This required larger boats with more engine power.

The pound net is a stationary net attached to poles and was introduced to the bay in the 1850s. The pound-net and haul seine fisheries are labor-intensive and require the use of multiple boats. Large and small deadrise boats are used in these fisheries.

Floating, staked, and anchored gill nets and fish pots came along later. The gill-net fisheries also played a role in the demand for deadrise boats as watermen worked longer nets that required larger boats to haul nets to fishing grounds and to carry home increased payload.

Spring, summer, and fall charter boat fishing provided work for those who owned deadrise boats. When the water warms enough for hook-and-line fishing, the "For Hire" signs went up and boats carried city folks out for a day of fishing. The extended roofline on the *Union* provided shade and protection from the weather. George and Thelma Mowbray display a catch of croaker they caught in 1946. (Courtesy of Buddy Wyker.)

During the 1960s hook-and-line cobia fishing brought many recreational fishermen to Deltaville, Virginia. This 1962 photograph was taken at Capt. Dewey Norton's Jackson Creek dock after a day of fishing aboard his wooden deadrise, *My Lady*. On November 18, 1963, Norton broke the Virginia hook-an-line saltwater record for landing the largest striped bass ever caught in the state. He held that record for 18 years. (Courtesy of Alva Bray)

These fishermen out of Water View, Virginia, in the 1940s had a good day fishing and showed off their catch to the camera. They are standing on a deadrise boat. Lifelong memories are captured on the day a big fish was landed. Interestingly, over time as the story was retold the fish got bigger and bigger. (Courtesy of Middlesex County Museum.)

Rob Ann Jay is a classic wooden deadrise charter boat vessel. Capt. Tim Haley of Hartfield, Virginia, has a six-pack charter boat license and fishes out of Deltaville, Virginia, in the Piankatank and Rappahannock Rivers and Chesapeake Bay. The bay's charter boat fleet is located throughout Maryland and Virginia. (Author's collection.)

During the 1940s and 1950s, large schools of croakers were caught by haul seine fishermen, the likes that had never been seen before. For some fishermen, it was a "strike-it-rich" time when fishermen caught enough fish in a week to buy a new car or to pay for materials to build a new home. (Courtesy of Grace Daniel.)

These fish were caught by haul seine in the 1940s. The haul seine net was brought to Virginia by early English settlers and is used to this day to harvest fish. Flat-bottom and deadrise skiffs are used in the fishery along with larger deadrise boats to haul the skiffs full of fish to shore and when moving nets to another location. (Courtesy of Middlesex County Museum.)

This was quite a catch by Gloucester County, Virginia, watermen who caught this load of croaker and spot in a haul seine. While some haul seine fishermen use small skiffs to bring in their catch to shore others, as shown in this photograph, use larger deadrise boats to carry payload back to the fish dock. (Author's collection.)

When fishing a pound net, the large deadrise boat, to the left, is used to hold one side of the fish pocket full of fish as fishermen in the skiff net the fish and drop the catch into the bottom of the big boat. Multiple boats are used in the Chesapeake Bay pound-net fishery to harvest fish, install nets in the spring, and dismantle nets at the end of the fishing season. (Author's collection.)

This photograph shows the pound-net boat *Four Sons* of White Stone, Virginia, loaded down with fish after a morning of fishing. Most fish caught that day were menhaden and were sold for bait to customers fishing crab pots. Some food fish were caught and sold to a fish house. (Author's collection.)

After a day of fishing a pound net in the Rappahannock River, Capt. Paul Somers of White Stone, Virginia, and crew are headed home on the *Four Sons*. The mast and boom are used to install pound poles in the bottom of the bay and to hold and maneuver a dip net used to transfer fish caught in the pound net into the *Four Sons*. (Author's collection.)

The wooden deadrise *Manfred L* out of Reedville, Virginia, was being worked here in the Potomac River pound-net fishery in the late 1980s. Owner Eddie Gaskins had the vessel rigged and ready to go out to set pound-net poles. Pound poles seen here are stacked on starboard and port sides of the *Manfred L* on what fishermen refer to as "brakes." (Author's collection.)

The deadrise hull of the *Martha Virginia* provided an ideal platform for setting pound-net poles in Maryland's Potomac River. The water was almost "slick calm" an ideal day for setting poles. Setting poles is labor intensive as it takes a four-man crew and caption to set up and pound the poles into the bottom of the river. (Author's collection.)

Eddie Gaskins and crew aboard the deadrise *Martha Virginia* are setting pound poles in the Potomac River. They set the pole upright and then drive it into the bottom of the river with a steel driver. With much controversy, pound nets were introduced to the bay by northern fishermen and went on to become a favorite gear of Chesapeake Bay watermen. (Author's collection.)

Smaller deadrise boats are also used to haul poles out to the fishing grounds. The *Ashley B* has a set of poles aboard for the installation of a shallow water net on the Rappahannock River. As this happens only in the early spring, this has become a rare scene on the bay as the pound-net fishery has been in decline. (Author's collection.)

These pine tree pound-net poles are lying in wait near docks in Reedville, Virginia. Deadrise boats are used to fish, install, and remove pound nets. Pound nets are a stationary form of gear used to harvest finfish. The gear was introduced to the bay in the 1850s. (Author's collection.)

The *Virginia Mae* was built by Paul S. Green of Deltaville, Virginia, in the 1940s. Zach Asburn and Herbert C. Boatman have been out working a pound net and are on their way home to Ocran, Virginia. The *Virginia Mae* was built before the days of pilothouses as the boat has a cabin but no pilothouse. (Courtesy of Jack and Barbara Ashburn.)

Pound-net fisherman Wilson Rowe of Gwynn's Island, Virginia, is selling bait from his skiff in the 1980s near the mouth of Piankatank River to local crab potters. During the crab-pot season, crabbers gathered near Rowe's pound net to buy fresh menhaden to bait their pots. (Author's collection.)

One method of installing pound poles in the river bottom is with a pile driver mounted on the side of a boat. The *Maid King* was used for this and the photograph shows a pile driver on the boat. The vessel is a classic wooden deadrise and still has an outside rudder and steering stick, which is a carryback to the days of sailboats. (Author's collection.)

Deadrise and flat-bottom skiffs, also called "towbats" and "bats" by some watermen, were often powered by sculling paddles. Wilson Rowe sculled daily out into Edwards Creek from shore to his pound-net boat *Linda R* that he had built in 1936 in Susan, Virginia. A wetted-down towel is draped over a sculling pin that aids Rowe in keeping the paddle and skiff on track. (Author's collection.)

This photograph of this fish camp was taken in 1932 on Davis Creek in Mathews County, Virginia. It shows a fleet of pound-net boats several of which have pile drivers mounted on the sides. There is a net house for storing nets and a net reel on the shore along with poles stacked on the shoreline. (Courtesy the *Gloucester-Mathews Gazette-Journal*.)

Shad fisherman John Morey on Poropotank River is on his way out into the York River to fish a stake gill net. The plywood barrier on the skiff keeps the weather and spray out of his face. A wooden pin on the bow is used to hold the net stationary while he pulls fish out of the mesh. Gill nets were introduced on the Chesapeake around 1838, and staked gill nets were one variation. (Author's collection.)

The fiberglass deadrise *Stepaside II* was built in 1989 by John Callomore of Deltaville, Virginia, to fish for catfish on the Sassafras River in Cecil County, Maryland. Catfish are harvested in fish pots, and the live fish are sold to pay lakes in Ohio, Indiana, New York, Pennsylvania, and Kentucky to stock lakes where customers come to pay to fish with hook and line. (Author's collection.)

Ruby E and *Margaret* can be seen here on Pepper Creek in Mathews County in 1931. The boats are called trap boats because they were used in the pound-net fishery and pound nets were often called trap nets. Lennie and Alton Smith operated a boatbuilding operation on the creek and it can be seen off in the distance with a boat on the shore. (Courtesy of the *Gloucester-Mathews Gazette-Journal.*)

The crews of the deck boats *Ellen Marie* and *Irene & Pearl II* are selling menhaden for bait to crab trotline fishermen at Sandbank Wharf in Mathews County, Virginia. The pound-net fishery was one of the main suppliers of bait for trotlining and later for the crab-pot fishery. (Courtesy of the *Gloucester-Mathews Gazette-Journal.*)

The *Mary Trew* is a classic Chesapeake Bay wooden deadrise boat used in the pound-net fishery. It was built in the 1940s by Gilbert White of Palmer, Virginia. White started his boatbuilding life as a log-canoe builder and was a pioneer in the evolution of cross-planked deadrise boats. (Author's collection.)

Three

OYSTER BOATS

Virginia's and Maryland's oyster fisheries played a major role in the growth of a bay-wide wooden deadrise boatbuilding industry. Generationally, bayside and seaside (Atlantic Ocean) oysters provided sustenance and for profit in the day-to-day life of bay families. Oyster scissor-like hand tongs were introduced to the bay around 1700. Short-handled eight-foot to fourteen-foot tongs, called nippers, were used to harvest oysters in shoal waters. Oystermen standing on washboards of larger log canoes or deadrise boats used 16-to-32-foot shaft tongs to harvest seed and market-size oysters. As the oyster fishery grew and there was more demand for bay oysters, watermen had to move out into deeper water to catch oysters. New England oystermen introduced the oyster dredge in the late 1700s—a deepwater gear. This overtime led to state laws that shaped the future and development of some styles of deadrise boats. Maryland's law required that a dredge can only be worked from a sail-powered vessel. This resulted in the growth of the State of Maryland's sailing skipjack fleet. As an outcome, Maryland, to this day, has the last commercial fishing sailing fleet in North America. The Virginia legislature authorized Lt. James Bowen Baylor of the US Coast and Geodetic Survey in the 1890s to survey 110,000 areas of oyster grounds to be used by private growers to grow oysters. Virginia law allowed the use of dredges from large motor-powered boats on private state-leased oyster grounds. This, in part, led to demand for large 50-to-80-foot deadrise boats, referred to as buyboats or deck boats. Today, Virginia law allows a small 22-inch-wide dredge on authorized public oyster bottoms. An oyster gear known as a "patent tong" was first patented in 1887 by Charles L. Marsh a blacksmith in Solomons, Maryland. A Virginia style with "right angle heads" was patented in April 1890 by Joseph A. Bristow of Stormont, Virginia, and blacksmith William M. Dixon of Mathews County, Virginia. Patent tongs allowed watermen in mid-range size boats to harvest oysters in deepwater and encouraged the development of the modern-day deadrise boat as a platform to work from.

By the early 1970s, deadrise oyster boats had evolved into the modern style with a pilothouse atop the house. These boats still carried several features of earlier wooden boats. The *Gladys*, *Mary C*, and *Falcon* all have squat boards, also called settling or planing boards, on sterns, and the boat at the far end has a V-stern, a carryback to pointed-ended log canoes. (Author's collection.)

The term "deadrise" is a relatively new term in the history of V-bottom/cross-planked boats on Chesapeake Bay. During the early years of sail and power, bateau was the name most used to describe today's deadrise boat. The boat in the front is a classic bateau, which is an open V-bottom boat with no house/pilothouse. The deck boat *Mobjack* is in the background. (Courtesy of the *Gloucester-Mathews Gazette-Journal*.)

An ancient way of harvesting oysters is with hand tongs. Hand tongs were introduced to the bay in the early 1700s and are still used today. These hand tongers are standing on washboards and tonging up oysters. Oysters are piled on the culling board. Usually, there is a "culling boy" who is paid to separate legal-size oysters from the catch. Small oysters are thrown overboard. (Author's collection.)

Roosevelt Wingfield hand tongs for oysters standing on washboards of his deadrise boat. Roosevelt was working alone on that day in the 1980s, and when his culling board was full of oysters, he would stop working the tongs and cull his oysters. When times were good, there was a culling man onboard so the tonger—and sometimes, two tongers—could work while the cull man culled. (Author's collection.)

This is a classic photograph showing the tonger and culling man working. Most oystermen started life on the river as culling boys. Young boys went to work on their father's or uncle's oyster boats to help earn money for the family. School was often secondary in life, and many young boys in the 19th and early 20th centuries quit school at an early age to go cull oysters. (Author's collection.)

Kent Island, Maryland, waterman James Ralph Lee demonstrates how he used a "power assist" hand tong system to harvest oysters on his deadrise boat named *Twilight*. A foot button built into the washboard releases and hauls up a hydraulic-powered line attached to the tong head. The device is legal in the state of Maryland but illegal in Virginia waters. (Author's collection.)

This photograph shows a foot button in the washboard and line that are part of a "power assist" hydraulic hand tong hauler. Charles A. "Jim" Fluharty Sr. of Tilghman Island, Maryland, invented the hauler. He retired from Tilghman Packing Co. in 1968 to go work the water. As he got older, he invented the hydraulic hand tong hauler so he could continue to work the water. Maryland's legislature approved the use of the power assist gear in the early 1980s. (Author's collection.)

This round-head oyster tong called "eel-pot heads" have a spring-loaded clip attached to the tong head, which enables the power-assist hydraulic gear to haul tongs full of oysters to the service. Eel-pot heads enable watermen to empty the catch through the sides without always having to open up the heads. (Author's collection.)

A single oysterman was working the deadrise *Star Baby* out of Weems, Virginia, in 1986. Working a pair of hand tongs was not an easy chore but a good tonger with a good boat could catch enough oysters over the season to provide for his family. When the season ended, oystermen often turned to some form of agriculture work or went to work in the summer fisheries. (Author's collection.)

Oyster tubs as shown in the bottom of this deadrise boat are an essential tool used in the Chesapeake Bay oyster trade. Maryland and Virginia tubs have different dimensions. A Maryland bushel tub is 16.5 inches across the bottom, 18 inches across the top, and 21 inches diagonally from the inside chine to the top. A Virginia bushel tub measures 18.5 inches across the top, 17 inches across the bottom, and 21.5 inches diagonally from the inside chine to the top. (Courtesy of John M. Bareford Jr.)

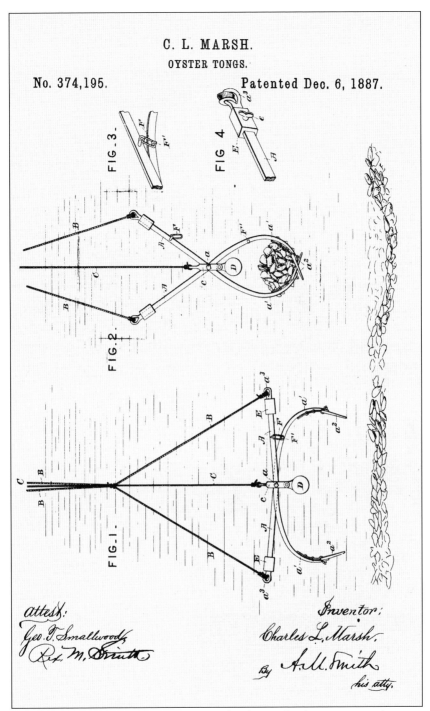

Blacksmith Charles L. Marsh of Solomons, Maryland, was the first to patent deepwater oyster tongs in 1887. The hand-powered patent tong invention was revolutionary and allowed oystermen to work on oyster grounds that had previously been in too deep of water for hand oyster tongs to reach. The invention quickly spread to Virginia where a variation of Marsh's tong was patented by two Virginians. (Courtesy of the US Patent Office.)

BRISTOW & DIXON

PATENTEES AND MANUFACTURERS OF

DEEP WATER OYSTER TONGS,

STORMONT, VIRGINIA.

The only rightangle heads, and consequently the only perfect working tongs invented.

The release brace being on top of the tongs it is always free to unlock and let the tongs close on the bottom.

The only tongs that the weights, or anchors, pull equally from each arm, and thereby prevent tripping or turning over while getting in the bivalves.

Can be used for taking Oysters, Clams, Muscles, Sponge or Coral in any depth of water.

Shipped to all parts of the World on short notice.

Joseph A. Bristow and William M. Dixon published this brochure in 1890 advertising that their Virginia deep-water tongs could be used to harvest oysters, clams, mussels, sponges, or coral. The Bristow & Dixon tongs won a blue ribbon at the 1898 Chicago World Fair. The main difference between the Virginia and Maryland styles of patent tongs was the shape of the tong head and the catch used to open and close the tongs. (Courtesy of John M. "Buddy" Moore.)

Oystermen on this fiberglass deadrise from Kilmarnock, Virginia, are working a pair of Virginia-style patent oyster tongs in the Rappahannock River. Patent tongs enabled oystermen to work in deeper water than hand tongs. This double patent tong rig was a bit unusual, as most watermen work just one tong, and the second man in the boat culls the oysters. (Author's collection.)

The patent oyster tong was a 19th-century gear that became even more effective in the 20th century. As deadrise boats grew in size and hydraulics evolved to haul tongs up and down, watermen went to working two patent tong rigs on a boat. Although seldom seen today, this photograph taken in the 1980s shows a closeup of a double patent tong rig. (Author's collection.)

Rental Receipts for Oyster Grounds.

$ 200   *INSPECTOR'S OFFICE,* Aug 17   190 8.

District No. 18 c Middlesex County, Va.

RECEIVED of J F Hughes the sum of
Two Dollars and Cents
for the rent of Two acres of Oyster planting grounds for the year ending the
1 day of Sept , 1909. Said ground is situated in the waters of
Lagrange Creek
and more particularly designated in the plat and survey recorded in the clerk's office of said county.

James S Chandler Inspector.

District No. 18 C

Virginia State Legislature agreed in 1894 to establish public and private oyster grounds in state waters. This allowed people to lease state grounds to grow their own oysters. John Hughes ran a general merchandise store at Street, Virginia, in 1908. He leased two shallow water acres of oyster ground near his home on Lagrange Creek. On his two acres, he grew oysters to sell at his store and to provide oyster stew on his dining room table. (Courtesy of Danny and Mary Loving.)

When Virginia legislators established private and public oyster grounds in the late 1890s a law was passed to allow the dredge to be worked on private state leased grounds from motor-powered boats. This dredge that holds twenty bushels is used today by Richard Green on the deck boat *Mobjack* to harvest oysters from grounds Green leases on the York and James Rivers. (Author's collection.)

A 22-inch-wide oyster dredge is being worked here on *Danny Boy* in the Rappahannock River. The use of the small dredge on public oyster rock is allowed during the oyster season on Virginia's rotational public beds. Virginia Marine Resources Commission rotates public oyster grounds every few years and when open for harvest these small dredges are allowed to work on the beds. (Author's collection.)

Todd Parks of Tangier Island, Virginia, works a 22-inch wide dredge in Virginia public oyster fishery. The small dredge accommodates the state-required eight-bushel limit per license. Usually, there are two men working a boat. If the other man has a license, the limit jumps to 16 bushels per boat and provides a full day of oystering. (Author's collection.)

This photograph is of the *Miss Margarett* and a fleet of boats rigged for the winter and fall oyster dredge season. A mast/boom is mounted as far forward as possible in the *Miss Margarett* and is removed during the off-season so the boat can be used for summertime recreational use. The

photograph was taken in December 1947 and shows a blending of styles of deadrise boats ranging from deck boats to classic bateaux. (Courtesy of Marcia Jones.)

Donald was a deadrise boat used by Harvey C. Smith of Sharps, Virginia, to dredge oysters. The vessel was confiscated from its owner in the early 1940s on the Potomac River by Virginia State Law Enforcement for illegal oystering. Ben Godfrey Smith of Sharps bought the boat from the state. This photograph was taken in 1949 at Sharps. (Courtesy of Marcia Jones.)

Large deadrise deck boats are used to purchase and plant seed oysters on public and private oyster grounds in Virginia and Maryland. Pictured here are the crew of the deck boat *Thomas W.* planting seed on state-leased oyster grounds while Virginia Marine Resources Police oversee the process. (Courtesy of the *Southside Sentinel*.)

Oyster shells are planted on creeks and coves to encourage the growth of oysters. Oysters are filter feeders, and one oyster can filter up to 50 gallons of water a day. The states of Maryland and Virginia are encouraging the planting of seed and shell to clean up the bay. The deadrise *Marion Rose* was used to tow this barge full of shell when planting on Urbanna Creek. (Author's collection.)

This fleet of deadrise boats is working in the Virginia public oyster dredge fishery on the Rappahannock River. The state of Virginia rotates the harvest times on public grounds every so many years for conservation reasons. There was a great decline in the oyster population on the bay in the 1980s and 1990s but due to concerted scientific and environmental efforts by Virginia and Maryland, oysters are coming back. (Author's collection.)

When the state of Virginia set limits at eight bushels a day per license, small deadrise skiffs like this one started working in the state's dredge fishery. More small boats are working in the fishery today than ever before because larger boats burn more fuel and are harder to maintain and an eight-bushel limit does not require the use of a big boat to carry the small payload to market. (Author's collection.)

Over his lifetime, boatbuilder Edward Diggs of Mathew County, Virginia, built a fleet of deadrise wooden boats for oyster, crab, and finfish fisheries. This *Diggs45* is one of his classic round-stern designs. Diggs, like most Chesapeake Bay boatbuilders, built his boats from "rake of eye" and never used plans. Diggs, along with Grover Lee Owens of Deltaville, Virginia, built some of the prettiest deadrise boats on the bay. (Author's collection.)

Francis Haynie of Northumberland County, Virginia, built wooden deadrise boats for the Potomac River oyster fishery. Haynie was one of the last bay boatbuilders who went out in the wood, marked his trees, and had them cut and planked for his boatbuilding business. Haynie is caulking the seams of one of his boats with an old-time caulking iron and hammer. (Author's collection.)

The sailing skipjack fleet is exclusive to Maryland's oyster fishery. The fleet is the only commercial working sailing fleet today in North America. Skipjacks were built to dredge oysters. This sailing skipjack is being repaired at Reedville Marine Railway in Reedville, Virginia, by yard owner George P. Butler. (Courtesy of Becky and George Butler.)

The deadrise V-bottom on the sailing skipjack *Claud W. Somers* is visible when it is up on the rails at Cockrell Marine Railway in Northumberland County, Virginia. Reedville Fishermen's Museum owns the 1911 *Claud W. Somers* and uses it as an education and charter boat. It is listed in the National Register of Historic Places and Virginia Register of Historic Places. (Author's collection.)

The *Claud W. Somers* has a classic outside sailing rudder. The sailing skipjack is still around because the Maryland legislature passed laws in the late 1800s requiring the use of a dredge to harvest oysters in boats under sail. A modification to the law came in 1967 when the legislature allowed the use of push boats to motor the skipjack on Monday and Tuesday. They are referred to as "power days." (Author's collection.)

These two skipjacks are racing at the annual Labor Day Deal Island, Maryland, skipjack races. Traditionally, watermen took pride in having the fastest boat. Whether under power or sail or oar, captains took pride in having bragging rights after beating fellow watermen to the finish line. (Courtesy of Hannah Straub.)

This photograph shows two skipjacks and a traditional deadrise boat between them. The V-deadrise hull and cross-planked bottom of the skipjack and the traditional motor-powered deadrise are basically built the same way. The deadrise hull evolved from the days of sail and transcended into the days of internal combustion engines. (Courtesy of Hannah Straub.)

The sails on this skipjack have a patch or two. During the days of sail, most neighborhoods in Tidewater Maryland and Virginia had a sailmaker to go along with the railway down on the shore. Before the internal combustion engine, sailmakers played an important role in the day-to-day life of working watermen and they do to this day for the skipjacks. (Courtesy of Hannah Straub.)

The *Caleb W. Jones* of Wenona, Maryland, was built in 1953 at C.H. (Herbert) Rice and Son Boatyard in Reedville, Virginia. Rice built boats on Cockrell Creek and built two other well-known skipjacks. He built the *City of Crisfield* in 1948 and *Somerset* in 1949. His yard specialized in building wooden purse boats for the menhaden fishery but he is best known for his skipjacks. (Author's collection.)

Rebecca T. Ruark was built in 1886 and is the oldest sailing skipjack-rigged vessel on the bay. She has a pungy hull, which is not of the cross-planked and deadrise style. On days when there is plenty of wind offshore, she can sail faster than most skipjacks but on a calm day with gusts of winds close to shore, the deadrise skipjack hull can sail passed the round bilged pungy. (Author's collection.)

Generations of watermen's hands have guided skipjacks out to Maryland's oyster grounds and brought the boats and crew home loaded down with oysters. Capt. Wade Murphy of *Rebecca T. Ruark* is a third-generation skipjack captain who still had his hands on the wheel in the 1980s. (Author's collection.)

Working a dredge is hard and often cold dangerous work. The crew of the *Rebecca T. Ruark* worked on deck just inches between the boat and the waters of the bay. This photograph shows raindrops falling on a cold, slippery day on the decks of the boat. The crew spent a lot of the day on their knees working. (Author's collection.)

On a Monday in the 1980s, the *Rebecca T. Ruark* was being powered by a motorized push boat. The sun finally broke through the sky and clusters of diamond-like images danced across the water—a sign that the bay had a softer face. Chesapeake Bay watermen daily face the environment that God's nature gives them. (Author's collection.)

The buyboat *Nellie Crockett* is loaded down with seed oysters in the early 1980s. Capt. James Ward had purchased seed from oyster hand tongers on the James River. The *Nellie Crockett* was built in 1925 and is in the National Register of Historic Places and National Historic Landmarks in Maryland. (Author's collection.)

The age-old method of planting seed oysters is by broadcasting shell across the grounds by using a shovel and strong arms. The modern method is to use a high-powered water hose to blow the oysters off the deck. Capt. James Ward used a five-man crew aboard the *Nellie Crocket* to shovel oysters onto oyster grounds. (Author's collection.)

The *Nellie Crocket* had 1,822 bushels of seed oysters on her this day, and it took five men an hour and a half to plant the seed by broadcasting seed with a shovel on Virginia leased oyster ground near Water View, Virginia, on the Rappahannock River. *Nellie Crocket* is owned today by Ted Parish of Georgetown, Maryland. (Author's collection.)

The *Grace* was a fore-and-aft bottom-planked deadrise boat built by Lepron Johnson of Crittenden, Virginia, in 1906. When this photograph was taken, *Grace* was owned by Clyde Green of Remlik, Virginia, who bought oysters for Buster Ferguson's oyster-shucking house in Remlik. (Courtesy of Marie Stallings.)

Capt. Johnny Ward of Deltaville, Virginia, was buying oysters from oystermen near the mouth of the Piankatank River in 1964. The photograph shows a variety of styles of deadrise boats from one with a rounded pilothouse to another with no pilothouse at all. Captain Johnny named the boat *Iva W.* after his wife. (Courtesy of John M. Bareford Jr.)

Deadrise boats and log canoes were used by oystermen to row out to George L. Smith's private oyster grounds near Sharps, Virginia, on the Rappahannock River. Oystermen were paid piecemeal, so much per bushel for the oysters, they caught that day. This photograph taken in the 1930s shows oystermen back at the dock after a long day of hand tonging. (Courtesy of Marcia Jones.)

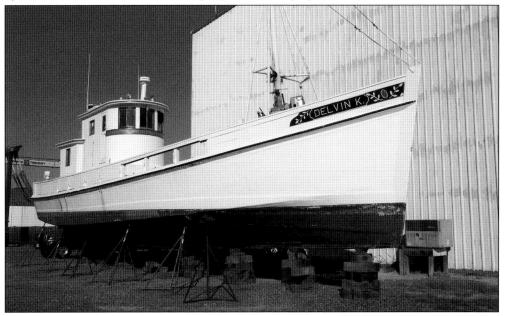

The *Delvin K.* is the last Chesapeake Bay buyboat on the bay used to buy oysters. Jerry Pruitt of Tangier Island, Virginia, buys oysters from watermen on the *Delvin K.* and hauls the load to a Reedville, Virginia, oyster buyer. *Delvin K.* was built in 1949 by Sidney Smith of Bena, Virginia. Deck boat–style deadrise boats are also called buyboats. (Author's collection.)

Capt. R.D. Ailsworth, atop the pilothouse, is keeping tally on the bushel tubs of oysters that are coming aboard his oyster buyboat the *Lillian T*. The tallyman had to keep count of the number of bushels and from which boat each bushel came. The 55-foot *Lillian T*. was built by Linwood Price of Deltaville in 1928. (Courtesy of Alfred E. Ailsworth Jr.)

Four

CRAB BOATS

Although the bay blue crab fishery is the youngest of the bay's three major fisheries, it is believed that the first deadrise and cross-planked boats on the bay were built for crabbing. When the railroad expanded down Maryland and Virginia's Eastern Shore in the 1800s, a bay-wide soft-shell crab fishery grew. The railroad provided a prompt avenue for shipping live soft-shell crabs to restaurants in Baltimore and Washington, DC. Tangier Sound was a shallow, aquatic grassy bottom ideal for catching peeler and soft-shell crabs. Watermen needed a hull style that provided enough stability to comfortably sail through deep water to arrive at the grounds and a shallow enough draft to work in the shoal waters. The V-bottom and cross-planked sailing skiff was the answer, and it is believed the style spread up and down the Eastern Shore of Maryland and Virginia and then to other areas of the bay. The internal combustible engine was introduced about the same time as deadrise construction came along. Boatbuilders were able to modify the deadrise style for either motor or sail power. One of the most unique deadrise boats that evolved from sail was the Barcat, also called a Smith Island scrape boat. The Barcat is a low-sided, shallow-draft deadrise used primarily for catching peelers and soft-shells with a scrape. The crab scrape was patented in 1870 by L. Copper Dize of Crisfield, Maryland. Barcats were specifically designed around the gear and shallow grassy bottom of Tangier Sound. Another early gear form used in harvesting hard-shell crabs was the trotline and dip-net. A trotline is a long line, anchored at both ends with bait attached every three feet on the line. Crab pots were first patented by Benjamine F. Lewis of Harryhogan, Virginia, in 1928. He revised the patent in 1938 and received another patent on what is today the modern crab pot. For a short while, in the 1980s and 1990s, bay boatbuilders went to building traditional deadrise boats in the 45-to-50-foot range to work dredges off the sterns of the boats in Virginia's winter crab dredge fishery. Prior to that, the boats were built in the 38-to-42-foot range. That window of boatbuilding opportunity lasted from about 1985 to 2008 when the Virginia Marine Resources Commission banned the winter dredge fishery for conservation reasons.

Those living near Tidewater Virginia and Maryland waters caught crabs with a crab net and a baited string. They enjoyed steamed hard crabs and fried soft-shell crabs on a daily basis in the summertime. The baited line on the string led to the commercial trotline fishery. (Courtesy of Betty Burton.)

This 1943 drawing of a crab trotline shows how a trotline is set in the water. The ends are anchored to the bottom and attached to barrel buoys at each end. The crab-line ends are also attached to the barrel. Bait is tied to the line, and watermen in a boat are settling in to wait for enough time to pass for crabs to grab hold of the bait. (Courtesy of Virginia Institute of Marine Science.)

Bobby "Tucker" Lee of Kent Island, Maryland, is fishing a classic style trotline in Maryland's Wye River. Lee is the son of Lester Lee, whom William Warner made famous in his Pulitzer Prize award-winning book on bay blue crabs entitled *Beautiful Swimmers*. Tucker uses a classic deadrise to fish his lines. He is laying out a trotline for a day of fishing. (Author's collection.)

Tucker Lee used an old car part that he got from a junkyard to anchor his trotline. The trotline was the main gear used by Maryland and Virginia watermen to harvest crabs until the crab pot came along in the late 1920s. Today, the trotline is still used in Maryland rivers where crab pots are banned for conservation reasons by the state legislature. (Author's collection.)

The trotline fishery supplies large jimmy (male) hard crabs for the bay's hard-shell basket market. Crabs are sold by the basket, or by the dozen, either steamed or not steamed so the customer can cook their own. The rivers of Maryland produce some of the largest jimmy crabs on Chesapeake Bay. (Author's collection.)

This photograph shows how this trotline crabber uses a cat-quick motion to dip the crabs off the trotline. The trotline is an 18th-century gear form on Chesapeake Bay that is still being used today to catch crabs. The classic deadrise boat is one of the main platforms used in this fishery. (Author's collection.)

When the crab pot was first patented in 1928 by Benjamin F. Lewis of Harryhogan, Virginia, watermen set stacks in the bottom of the river and tied pots to it as shown in this photograph. They later changed to rigging pots by tying one end of a line to the pot and the other end to a buoy that floated to the surface to mark the location. (Author's collection.)

When watermen started fishing crab pots, they pulled the pots by hand. Later, hydraulic pot haulers, like the one in this photograph, came along. Ed Payne and his son Henry are fishing pots in the 1980s in a deadrise skiff. Small deadrise boats work well in the crab-pot fishery, particularly when watermen fish in protected waters. (Author's collection.)

This deadrise skiff was built by Edward Diggs of Mathews County, Virginia. Diggs grew up among boatbuilders and started as a boy blowing sawdust off his father's saw mark. When he was 16 years old, he went to work full-time building boats with his father and uncle Ned Hudgins. (Author's collection.)

For watermen who have a Virginia 450 crab pot license, a larger deadrise boat is preferred. The *Miss Barbara* of Hayes, Virginia, is a 42-foot-by-12-foot classic deadrise that is worked in the crab-pot fishery. The platform on the stern is used to haul and move crab pots from one location to another. Watermen are offloading their catch at Benny Belvin's crab house in Perrin, Virginia. (Author's collection.)

The late Benny Belvin ran a seafood house in Perrin for many years. There, he bought crabs and supplied bait to crabbers. A crab buyer plays an important role in the life of bay watermen and their boats. Stray cats are also part of the seafood culture and are found around most seafood houses. Benny loved his cats and provided a seafood dish for them daily. (Author's collection.)

When a waterman ages, it is often hard to give up working the water. The late Paul Pruitt in his youth was captain of the deck boat *P.E. Pruitt*, which he had built in Crisfield, Maryland, in 1935. When he got old, he bought a little deadrise that he named *Ruth* after his wife. As seen in this photograph, she had a sweet little roundhouse on her. (Courtesy of *Southside Sentinel*.)

Charles Charnock & Son bait and ice business on Tangier Island, Virginia, was an essential and convenient business for the island's crab potters. On-the-water bait houses allow crabbers to pull their crab boats right up to the dock and buy bait and ice for a day's work. (Author's collection.)

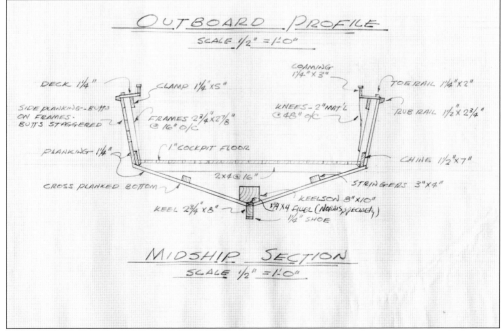

Alfred Norris built boats in Deltaville, Virginia, from rack of eye, without using formal plans. In 1964, boatbuilder Joe Conboy was working at Price's Railway in Deltaville and spent some time with Norris at his boat shop on Lovers Lane. Conboy drew rough plans of Norris's deadrise boats. Norris also built numerous boats for crab-pot fishermen. (Courtesy of Joe Conboy.)

Tangier Island, Virginia, crab shanties are built out on the water where island crabbers store their pots, moor their boats, shed crabs, and conduct the day-to-day business that surrounds the life of an island crabber. On a good day, a visitor might catch an islander's wife at the shanty cooking

up some crab stew. This is made in a big pot with the backs, aprons, and dead man's fingers (gills) removed from hard-shell crabs. The crabs are dropped into a boiling pot mixed with corn on the cob, potatoes, onions, and whatever else the cook desires and boiled until ready. (Author's collection.)

The *Margaretta II* and *Two Girls* are examples of classic deadrise boats. *Margaretta II*, with its sweeping bow, is used in the Tangier Island crab-pot fishery. The island is one of the few places on the bay where stacks and stacks of crab pots can be seen along the shoreline. The *Two Girls* is a deadrise Barcat used to scrape for crabs in Tangier Sound. (Author's collection.)

The *Margaret H* is a classic Smith Island crab scrape boat. She was built by Smith Island, Maryland, boatbuilder Lawson Tyler in the 1960s. The same style of boat was used in the days of sail to harvest crabs. Capt. Edward Harrison, in the boat, has owned two boats of this style. The first was built for sail in Norfolk, Virginia. When that boat had seen better days, Harrison had the *Margaret H* built for power and named it after his daughter. (Author's collection.)

The crab scrape was patented in 1870 by L. Copper Dize of Crisfield, Maryland. Some maritime historians believe that the deadrise and cross-planked style of boat may have evolved in part out of the need to develop a boat for this new crab scrape fishery. The scrape is hand-pulled and designed to catch peeler and soft-shell crabs in extremely shallow water of Tangier Sound, where crabs go to shed or molt in the grassy bottom. (Author's collection.)

The tools used in the crab scrape business include a scrape, a wooden crab carry float, a dip net, and a long knobby piece of driftwood used to mark submerged tree trunks. Also, an occasional friend comes along on the trip, as a black-headed laughing gull stops by, awaiting a tasty bite of whatever might surface from the dredge. (Author's collection.)

The *Carol Lynn* is a classic Smith Island, Maryland, scrape boat. The boat is used to scrape for peeler and soft-shell crabs. This 1989 photograph shows the onshore shedding facility where peeler crabs were brought and placed in molting tanks for the crabs to shed into soft shells. On Smith Island, most shedding facilities are built on the marshy guts along the island shores. (Author's collection.)

Miss Angel is a Smith Island, Maryland, double scrape boat with a standard house/pilothouse built forward. Most crab-scape boats are open boats, which provide more work and payload space for the crabber. Over the generations, deadrise boat owners have tweaked the styles to accommodate their own needs in a boat. (Author's collection.)

Capt. Edward Harrison checks the sign on a peeler crab that determines the stage of molting. The three stages are green, medium, and ripe, with green peelers just beginning to shed, medium about halfway, and ripe peelers just hours away from turning into soft-shell crab. When the hard shell begins to break away from the body of the crab it is called a buster crab. (Author's collection.)

When sold to a restaurant, this large soft-shell crab is referred to as a whale. Crabs distinctively go to shallow grassy water bottom to find safety when they go through molting stages to protect them from predators. Every time the crab molts its exoskeleton, it grows in size. (Author's collection.)

On Virginia's York River, waterman John Morey works in a small skiff, catching peeler crabs in peeler pounds. A peeler pound is a stationary trap with a wire leader that extends from shore to a box-like trap into deeper water. When the crab touches the leader it distinctively goes to deeper water winding up inside the trap. Morey is sorting his catch and will take the crabs back to his shedding facility at his home. (Author's collection.)

This photograph is of a waterman culling peeler crabs at a crab dock on Gwynn's Island, Virginia, sometime in the 1980s. When crabs are caught and then dumped into the bottom of a boat, it can result in quite a scramble. The three baskets are to separate the green, medium, and ripe peeler crabs from one another. (Author's collection.)

On Tangier Island, scrape boats are called Barcats, and this one is equipped with a radio to provide music while the crabber is working. The wooden box attached to the awning platform aft keeps the radio out of the weather. Tangier Sound, between Tangier, Smith, South Marsh, and Deal Islands, is considered some of the best crabbing grounds on Chesapeake Bay. (Author's collection.)

The worn and weathered image on the center tombstone of the late David Tyler shows an embossment of a sailing skipjack. The tombstone reads that David was born July 28, 1871, and died February 10, 1904. This was during the time period that deadrise and cross-planked construction evolved on the bay. The silent voice of this Smith Island cemetery speaks of generations of islanders who worked the water in deadrise boats. (Author's collection.)

The shoal waters of Tangier Sound and shallow, grassy waters along Virginia and Maryland Eastern Shore may have sparked a boatbuilding revolution that has lasted for nearly 150 years. Although no one knows for certain who built the first deadrise and cross-planked bottom boat on the

bay, maritime historian Howard Chapelle speculated that the origin of the deadrise boats today may have started from small sailing skiffs built on the Eastern Shore of Maryland and Virginia. (Author's collection.)

The winter crab dredge fishery was banned in 2008 by Virginia in an effort to preserve the bay's blue crab population. This 1977 photograph shows a fleet of dredge boats working in Chesapeake Bay. Traditionally deck boats, like *Olive Virginia*, worked exclusively in the fishery and pulled two dredges from the sides. Later, watermen modified sterns on smaller deadrise boats so two dredges could be worked off the stern. (Courtesy of Carlos Smith.)

The deadrise deck boat *Ward Brothers* is shown here dredging crabs near the edge of the Chesapeake Bay cut channel. Virginia dredge boats worked right up against the channel in the winter crab dredge fishery. In the background, a large tanker passes by on its way to Baltimore, Maryland. (Author's collection.)

Capt. Floyd Ward and the crew of the deck boat *Thomas W.* are off-loading barrels of crabs from his father's boat named *Iva W.* after a day of crabbing dredging. Johnny Ward of Deltaville, Virginia, and his three sons owned numerous deadrise deck boats over the years, and the family worked in the crab dredge fishery until it was banned in 2008. (Author's collection.)

The business of working a crab dredge is dangerous work. Although the dredge is mechanically driven, the crew has to lift the dredge onto the deck of the boat and then shake the crabs out of the dredge. It is winter—cold and slippery—and on some days, the bay is unforgiving, making the day long and hard. (Author's collection.)

The dredge post holds the four chains that go to the dredges. When the season ends, some watermen take the dredge post out so they can use their boats for other endeavors. The crew of the *Iva W.* is in the process of corralling the crabs into baskets so they can be dumped into barrels. (Author's collection.)

When cold weather arrives, the Chesapeake Bay blue crab moves to deeper water into the lower bay and buries in the mud. The majority of the crabs caught in the winter dredge fishery, about 80 percent, were female which in part was the logic behind banning the fishery in 2008 when there were signs the crab population was declining. (Author's collection.)

The winter crab dredge fishery was the last avenue of work in the commercial fishing business for large deadrise deck boats. The 1880s deadrise and cross-planked hull style had evolved from small sailing skiffs to large 60-foot-and-over deck boats. The Ward Brothers, seen here in the 1980s, dredging for crabs was in her final stage of commercial fishing life. (Author's collection.)

The *Ann French* was built by Jerry Pruitt of Tangier Island for the winter crab dredge fishery. Some of the largest traditional-style house/pilothouse deadrise boats were built in the 1980s and 1990s for the dredge fishery. In the 1960s, watermen began to experiment by dragging two dredges from the stern of the smaller traditional deadrise boats. It worked, and the fishery moved away from using deck boats. (Author's collection.)

The smaller deadrise boats in the crab dredge fishery were more fuel efficient and two dredges off the stern worked as well as pulling two from the sides of the larger deck boat. The *Ann French* sports a polished mahogany stern a feature that watermen began having built into their boats in the 1980s and 1990s. A good-looking boat has been part of the bay's maritime culture for generations. (Author's collection.)

Five

SOUTHERN MARYLAND BOATS

The north bank of the Potomac River was one of the most interesting boatbuilding regions on Chesapeake Bay and home to the Potomac River dory. The dory is a fore-and-aft bottom-planked vessel that boatbuilders on the bay refer to as long-planked boats. It was a competitor of deadrise/cross-planked bottom boats and was around during the same time period. Like the Virginia deadrise, the modern dory started in the days of sail and was later modified to accommodate the internal combustion engine. The forerunner of the dory was a flat-bottom sailing craft called a "Nancy." The Nancy was sometimes referred to as "Black Nancy" because watermen often painted boats black using pine tar pitch from pine trees abundant on the north bank of the Potomac. The Nancy was used on the Potomac as far back as the colonial period. Like the dory, the Nancy had stem-to-stern bottom planking. The modern V-bottom dory evolved from the Nancy. One of the main visible differences between the dory and cross-planked deadrise boats is that the chine on a cross-planked deadrise usually runs slightly below the waterline and is flat through most of its run, rising only slightly forward. The dory has a distinct high, sweeping chine line in the sides and bow.

The *Jeanne S.* is a traditional Virginia-built deadrise and cross-planked vessel showing the hard chine line in the bow just above the waterline. The Potomac River dory *Lillian B* shows off the sweeping hard chine line in the bow that comes with fore-and-aft bottom planking. (Courtesy of Gary Thimsen.)

Sea Mist III shows off the pronounced Potomac River dory's sweeping chine line. Dories were mostly associated with Maryland's north bank of the Potomac River, but some dories were built on Virginia's south bank. Northumberland County, Virginia, boatbuilder, Francis Haynie said that he built one for a customer and he knew of other Virginia builders who had built one or two. (Author's collection.)

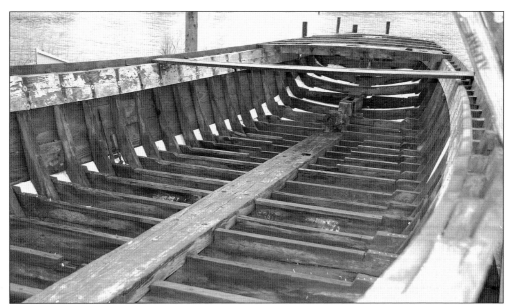

This photograph shows the interior bilge frame construction technique on the fore-and-aft bottom-planked Potomac River dory. The framing extends across the bottom so that the longitudinal planking can be attached and stiffened. The stem-to-stern planking is called "long planking" by Southern Maryland boatbuilders. (Author's collection.)

This photograph is of the interior of a traditional Deltaville, Virginia–built deadrise and cross-planked hull with two stringers, called "sister keelsons," giving stiffness to the bottom. It shows the contrast between the framing techniques in the bottom of a Potomac River dory (seen in the top image) and the Virginia-built deadrise and cross-planked boat. (Courtesy of Joe Conboy.)

The Potomac River dory *Laura* in this photograph shows off her house/pilothouse layout when she was being used in the Potomac River charter boat fishery. The *Laura* here is out in front in a race in the 1980s at Swann's Pier at Piney Point, Maryland. She was powered by a 455 Oldsmobile engine. (Courtesy of Danny Holden.)

The *Laura* was recently converted from a charter boat to a commercial hook-and-line fishing boat. The 38-foot boat was built in 1970 by Perry A. Gibson at Avenue, Maryland, and has been owned by the Holden family since 1974. Capt. Bobby Holden used the boat as a six-pack charter boat. Bobby's son Danny converted the boat to a commercial hook-and-line fishing boat. (Author's collection.)

The dory boat *Clipper* is being worked in the Potomac River crab pot fishery. It was built by Herman W. "Bill" Dixon of Abell, Maryland, on St. Patrick Creek. Dixon referred to his style of workboat as the "Potomac River Slider" because, according to him, his boats "slide across the water so fast." (Courtesy of Danny Holden.)

This pilothouse style on the Potomac River dory, *Clipper*, with a windshield-style front window and two sliding windows on the sides, was not unusual in Virginia or Maryland. However, pilothouse styles varied up and down the bay with builders. A boat's house/pilothouse style could often identify the boatbuilder who built the boat. (Courtesy of Danny Holden.)

Madness was built by Perry Aloysius Gibson in 1971. He built square-stern boats using the long planking style. Gibson later started building boats with cross-planked bottoms. *Madness* was restored in 2008 by Danny Holden in Avenue, Maryland. When this photograph was taken Madness was being used in the Potomac River blue crab fishery. (Courtesy of Danny Holden.)

Gone Fishing was built by Perry Gibson for the six-pack charter boat fishery and is a cross-planked bottom boat. Gibson built boats in Avenue, Maryland. The flare and rake in the sides of his boats were achieved by using a striped planking method of construction using narrow planks. (Courtesy of Danny Holden.)

Miss Jo Ann is a classic long-planked dory-style workboat. The future of wooden boats on the bay today is bleak as most of the men who built the boats have gone to heaven and the neighborhood boatyards where wooden boat owners brought their boats for maintenance and repair are gone. (Courtesy of Danny Holden.)

The dory *Nancy B.* was built by George Garner Gibson of Avenue, Maryland. Gibson was born in 1900 and learned the trade from his neighbor John Cheseldine who owned a boatyard near the mouth of Whites Neck Creek. Cheselfine was a well-known dory builder. Owner Robert T. Brown, seen here, worked the boat in the Potomac River pound-net fishery. (Author's collection.)

This long-planked dory-style boat was built in 1957 in Southern Maryland. The boat may have been a one-off build by a one-time boatbuilder or neighborhood builder who turned out just a few boats, as the hull is made from a variety of local wood including cherry, walnut, and other hardwoods. Cherry and walnut would be unusual boatbuilding lumber for use at a traditional boatyard. (Author's collection.)

The stern on this dory is a variation of sterns found on traditional sail-powered dory boat. This stern does have a similar "shield" shape found on early dory boats. Variations of traditional styles of sterns and other aspects were built into boats by builders who used their own one-off styles to build their boats. (Author's collection.)

Maryland builder Francis R. Goddard built over 150 boats in his lifetime but he is most noted for the two skipjacks he built. In 1979, he built the 56-foot sailing skipjack *Dee of St. Mary's* and, in 1984, the 56-foot skipjack *Connie Francis*. He also has the distinction of having built the last commercial buyboat built on the bay in the 20th century in 1989. (Author's collection.)

Cathy Lynn was built and rigged for Maryland's six-pack charter boat fishery. She was built by Piney Point, Maryland, boatbuilder Francis R. Goddard one of the most prolific Southern Maryland builders. He was a Potomac River boatbuilder who built in the deadrise and cross-planked bottom style. (Courtesy of Danny Holden.)

Bill Trossback Jr. of Drayden, Maryland, was a waterman/farmer in St. Mary's County, Maryland. He built boats for his own use and for relatives. He was part of a long tradition of working watermen who taught themselves to build and maintain wooden boats for their own use. (Courtesy of Danny Holden.)

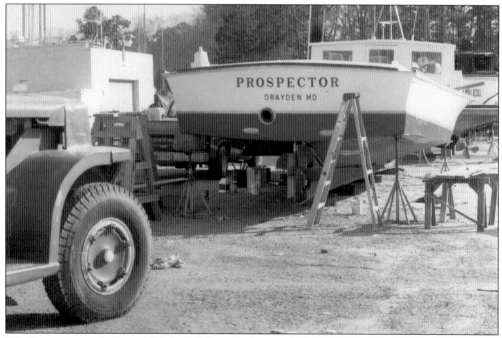

The *Prospector* was built in 1982 by Bill Trossback Jr. with the help of his sons Jimmy and Buddy. *Prospector* was used in the Potomac River eel pot and hydraulic clam fisheries. The boat has considerable flare in the sides, a cross-planked bottom, and a square stern. (Courtesy of Danny Holden.)

Francis R. Goddard also built the *Foxy Lady*, which was covered in snow in this photograph. Other well-known deadrise boats built by Goddard were *Daddy Frank, Susan Gail, Bushwacker,* and *Miss Jeanette.* Goddard's son Wayne learned the trade from his father and finished off the 46-foot *Miss Jeanette* in 1992, the last large boat built by Francis. (Courtesy of Danny Holden.)

The *Laura* was built by Perry Gibson. Danny Holden, who rebuilt the boat, said, "Mr. Gibson was an artist in the since that he understood the nature of wood and he shaped his hulls into a work of art." Gibson was one of several in his family who built boats in Southern Maryland. (Author's collection.)

At his railway on St. George River in Piney Point, Maryland, the late Francis Goddard holds his cat Tom Cat, who he named the boat he is standing in for. Goddard built his first boat, a 16-foot skiff, using wood off the side of his father's tobacco barn and went on to be one of Southern Maryland's most prolific boatbuilders. (Author's collection.)

This is a gathering of Potomac River boats participating in workboat races on St. George Creek at Piney Point, Maryland. The social gathering of boats is a tradition that goes back generations. The wooden dory boats in the photograph are *Hustler*, *Holly Elizabeth*, *Six Pack*, and *Miss Jo Ann*. There are several others that cannot be identified. (Courtesy of Danny Holden.)

Audrey B was built by Herman "Bill" Dixon and according to local lore, Dixon turned out four boats in a row similar to *Audrey B*. He had enough "scrap" materials left to build one more boat so he built the *Audrey B* with the leftover lumber. This is a classic square-stern, flared-bow dory-style boat. (Courtesy of Danny Holden.)

The *Nancy B* is seen here in Avenue, Maryland, when she was working in the Potomac River pound-net fishery. The dory and deadrise boats were used for work and play each in the same way. Why boatbuilders on the north bank of the Potomac River did not all switch to deadrise and cross-planked boatbuilding construction is simply most likely tied to tradition. (Author's collection.)

Southern Maryland has the distinction of having had the last bay deck boat built in the 20th century for commercial fishing on Chesapeake Bay. The *Poppa Francis* was built in 1989 by Francis Goddard. The heyday of bay deck boat construction was in the 1920s and 1930s, and prior to the *Poppa Francis*, the last one that had been built was in the 1970s. Goddard built the *Poppa Francis* to plant seed oysters and shell for the State of Maryland. (Author's collection.)

Six

REFLECTIONS

When the deadrise and cross-planked style was first introduced to the bay in the 1880s, over time boatbuilders from Chesapeake City, Maryland, to Virginia Beach, Virginia, joined in this grand experiment to change a bay-wide culture that had survived for centuries building boats out of logs. By the early 20th century, log boat construction had reached its pinnacle, and good boatbuilding logs were getting harder and harder to find. There was a demand for a new-style boat to take its place. The Chesapeake Bay deadrise was the answer and it changed the dynamics of maritime life on the bay. Deadrise planked boats could be built relatively inexpensively, which meant many households could afford a good boat. A good boat enabled families to improve their quality of life by being able to use the boat in a variety of different commercial endeavors. The boats also provided a good platform for day-to-day life, whether in a 12-foot deadrise skiff for children to cross the creek to visit the country store or in a larger boat for the family to cross the cove on Sunday to go to church. The success of the boats was in part because the wooden V-shaped deadrise in the bow of the boat was a good fit for the choppy seas in the protected waters of the bay. The bay's culture was also oriented to using wood as a boatbuilding material. Virginia and Maryland watermen were a long time coming around to accepting steel and fiberglass as boatbuilding materials. Even when these materials began to make headway in the 1970s, wooden boatbuilders were finding better ways to build boats. Although the lack of quality boatbuilding lumber became an issue, fasteners were improving. West System Epoxy, stainless steel bolts, and Monel nails came along in the 1970s, improving the finished boat. The decline of the Virginia wooden deadrise boat became evident in the 1990s as the cost of building a wooden boat came closer to the cost of building a fiberglass boat and boat owners began to move towards fiberglass hulls. The nail in the coffin of the Chesapeake Bay deadrise, however, has come as the people with the knowledge and talent to build the boats went to the local graveyards. With few with talent and knowledge coming behind them, the end of deadrise and cross-planked construction on a commercial level is in sight. These reflections of the past will someday be all there is of a once-booming commercial wooden boatbuilding industry on the bay.

The late Shelton "Shelly" Rowe of Gwynn's Island, Virginia, stands on the stern of the deadrise *Darnell* in 1990. Shelly and his brother Julian ran Shelly Rowe Seafood at Callis Wharf on Milford Haven. They fished pound nets and sold food fish to fish dealers and menhaden to crab potters for bait. (Courtesy of the *Gloucester-Mathews Gazette-Journal*.)

Mason Pugh (left) and Fielding Tillage, both of Port Haywood, Virginia, are off-loading shad and herring in March 1968. The two men are pound-net fishermen and fished nets in wooden deadrise boats. The spring run of shad and herring was the start of the fishing season. As summer and fall came, spot, croaker, menhaden, and bluefish became the fish of choice for pound-net fishermen. (Courtesy of the *Gloucester-Mathews Gazette-Journal*.)

When this photograph was taken of Bayside Wharf in Bavon, Virginia, there was a fleet of deadrise boats working in commercial fishing activities that were going on at the wharf. Bayside Wharf was a steamboat stop prior to 1933 when the steamboats stopped coming and in 1954 Hurricane Hazel destroyed the wharf. (Courtesy of the *Gloucester-Mathews Gazette-Journal*.)

The beauty of deadrise boats often attracted the eye and brushes of artists. This Mathews County, Virginia, art class was at Williams Wharf in 1955 capturing the images of buyboats and trawl boats. During the 1980s and 1990s, the artwork of John Barber and Franklin Saye adorned the walls of thousands of waterfront homes with their paintings and prints of bay boat scenes. (Courtesy of the *Gloucester-Mathews Gazette-Journal*.)

This photograph shows an early engine-powered deadrise boat with the Butler family of Reedville out for a Sunday afternoon ride. Engine boxes were not standard on the early boats. When underway, engines were often open to the air and covered with a tarp when at the dock to keep off the elements. The boy and man are at the steering stick attached to an "outside" rudder, a carry back to sailing days when boats were steered with a hand tiller. The ladies are dressed like they had just come from church. (Courtesy of Becky and George Butler.)

This 1950 photograph is of the round-stern *Jean Mae* loaded down with seed oysters. This scene is at Callis Wharf on Gwynn's Island, Virginia. *June* is a trap boat used in the pound-net fishery. The difference between a trap boat and a deck boat is that the house on a trap boat sits down on the floorboards of the boat, while the house on a deck boat is raised up higher on the deck. (Courtesy of the *Gloucester-Mathews Gazette-Journal*.)

This 1932 photograph is of men working on pound poles at Davis Creek. Deadrise boats can be seen along the waterfront in the background. The pound-net fishery was labor-intensive and required several types and sizes of wooden boats. The men in the photograph are scraping bark from the poles. (Courtesy of the *Gloucester-Mathews Gazette-Journal*.)

This photo was taken in the 1980s of the crew of the deadrise workboat *Hard Times* tonging oysters on the Rappahannock River. Hand shaft oysters tongs were introduced on the Chesapeake in the early 1700s and have been used to this day to harvest oysters. The major change in the gear was that in the 1700s the tong heads were made of wood instead of metal as they are today. (Author's collection.)

The *Pet* is a deadrise boat used in the pound-net fishery. She has a mast on her and an awning that looks like a sail. The awning is used to shade the fish when in the bottom of the boat and to keep the sun off of fishermen. The *Pet* has a V-style stern, which is called by some a Poquoson stern, most likely because the V stern was popular in that area of the bay. (Courtesy of the *Gloucester-Mathews Gazette-Journal*.)

Deadrise boats were not all about work. At the Labor Day boat races in 1955 on Urbanna Creek, there are two deadrise boats in the distance for the folks on the boats to watch the races. One of the boats is a classic round-stern workboat while the other is a party-boat style used to carry fishing parties out to hook and line fish. (Courtesy of Pat Marshall.)

The Blake sisters, of Topping, Virginia, are aboard their father's deadrise boat. Raymond Blake used his deadrise boat to hand tong for oysters in the winter and carry fishing parties in warm weather months. Blake was an oysterman/farmer. When his fields of watermelons were ripe, he filled the boat with melons, went across the river, and sold the watermelons off the boat to workers at a menhaden plant in White Stone, Virginia. (Courtesy of Emily Chowning.)

The trap boat *Betty Page* is under construction at Lennie and Alton Smith's boatyard on Pepper Creek in Mathews County, Virginia. The boat was built in 1931 and was fifty-eight feet by thirteen feet by four feet, eight inches. It was owned by pound-net fisherman Henry Owens. This photograph shows the structural elements of the boat, including two bulkheads, a keel, and sister keelsons in the bilge. (Courtesy of the *Gloucester-Mathews Gazette-Journal*.)

The *Betty Page* on launch day in 1931. Lennie and Alton Smith of Susan, Virginia, built hundreds of deadrise boats like the *Betty Page* for the pound-net fishery. This style of boat was built exclusively for pound-net fishing. Many trap boats, however, were later converted to deck boats and used in other fisheries. (Courtesy of the *Gloucester-Mathews Gazette-Journal*.)

This sweet, little round-stern deadrise was likely being used as a judge's boat for some type of race or event. If not maybe the men are on the way to church as they are dressed for a Sunday go-to meeting event. Many Tidewater families had a family boat, like this one, for pleasure and transportation. (Courtesy of the *Gloucester-Mathews Gazette-Journal*.)

The faces of young and old can be seen in this photograph at a fish house in the early 1930s. The fish house was a busy place. People came by boat to sell their catch and customers came by automobile to buy fish. In the top right corner, there is a car and a couple of gas pumps for customers to fill up with gas and watermen to buy gas for their boats. (Courtesy of the *Gloucester-Mathews Gazette-Journal*.)

Edna McLain was built in 1932 by Sidney and Jim Smith of Perrin, Virginia. The fish caught that day in the pound net were offloaded into the hold of the *Edna McLain* and sold to a fish house on the shore. Working a pound net is labor intensive as it takes a crew of men to bring the fish pocket to the surface and transfer the fish from the net into the boat, (Courtesy of the *Gloucester-Mathews Gazette-Journal*.)

When catches are small, fish are carried home in towboats, as shown here in this photograph. The flat-bottom skiffs are also called "seine skiffs" in some areas of the bay called "bats," an abbreviation of "towbat." The fishermen are likely waiting in line to sell to a fish house. (Courtesy of the *Gloucester-Mathews Gazette-Journal*.)

The buyboat *Birdie H* was built in Deltaville, Virginia, in 1934. One of the deadrise boats in the photograph has an outside rudder which is a carry back to the days of sail. The other boats are wooden flat-bottom towbats used in the pound-net fishery. (Courtesy of the *Gloucester-Mathews Gazette-Journal*.)

This photograph was taken at Davis Creek in Mathews County, Virginia, in the 1970s. There are two wooden deadrise skiffs up against the deck boat *Miss Lana*. The larger boats are working in Virginia's winter crab dredge fishery that was banned in 2008. Davis Creek was a hub of activity during the winter dredge season. (Courtesy of the *Gloucester-Mathews Gazette-Journal*.)

Virginia's winter crab dredge fleet was iced in during a winter freeze in 1973. The crab dredge fishery was the last fishery on the bay to provide work for the large bay deck boats. When the fishery was banned, many of the old workhorses were converted into pleasure boats. (Courtesy of the *Gloucester-Mathews Gazette-Journal*.)

The roundhouse *Chesapeake* is being worked in the bay's haul seine fishery. The men in the water are setting an anchor end of the haul seine so that the men in the boat can haul the other end out into the water. The ancient haul seine net was brought to Virginia with the first English settlers. (Courtesy of the *Gloucester-Mathews Gazette-Journal*.)

Renowned Virginia boatbuilder Edward Diggs, right, is building a deadrise boat at his boat shop at Horn Harbor Marina in Port Haywood, Virginia. Most bay boatbuilders built the hull and bottom of deadrise boats upside down, as shown in this photograph. When the bottom is completed, the boat is flipped over so that the top work can be installed. (Courtesy of the *Gloucester-Mathews Gazette-Journal*.)

Miss Margarett was named after the wife of George L. Smith of Sharps, Virginia. The boat was used to dredge oysters on Smith's private oyster grounds. This photograph was taken in August of 1947 when the dredge season had ended. The mast/boom used to dredge oysters had been removed and the boat was ready for summertime family cruising and recreational fishing. She was built in Deltaville, Virginia. (Courtesy of Marcia Jones.)

This fleet of wooden flat-bottom oyster skiffs worked on the Rappahannock River out of Sharps, Virginia. This photograph was taken in the 1930s showing C.B. Self and George L. Smith inspecting the boats. Oyster packing houses often provided boats and tongs for oystermen and paid them "piecemeal" per bushel of oysters caught. Deadrise skiffs were also used in this aspect of the oyster business. (Courtesy of Marcia Jones.)

This deadrise deck boat is offloading fish at Fairport Packing Co. in Reedville, Virginia. When fishing was big on the Chesapeake, fish houses were large and usually located down on the waterfront where boats could easily access the pier. The fish house supported the boats and the boats supported the fish house. (Courtesy of the Dr. A.L. VanName Jr. Collection, Deltaville Maritime Museum.)

During the heyday of Chesapeake Bay deck boats, there were several thousand of these boats on the bay. There are less than 50 left today with most of the boats have been converted to pleasure and education boats. Although most were built for commercial endeavors, there are just a few left being used for that today. (Courtesy of the Dr. A.L. VanName Collection, Deltaville Maritime Museum.)

This photograph taken at Conrad Steamboat Wharf on the Piankatank River shows a steamboat, a sailing schooner, and a deadrise deck boat loaded with watermelons. Deadrise deck boats were used extensively in the bay's watermelon trade. Melons were hauled to Washington, DC, or Baltimore, Maryland, and sold retail to walk-up customers at the docks. (Courtesy of Nola Watson.)

A wooden deadrise passes by this steam engine–powered yacht named *Remlik*. The yacht was owned by millionaire tycoon Willis Sharpe Kilmer of Binghamton, New York, and "Remlik" is "Kilmer" spelled backward. The folks in the deadrise most likely had spent the day on the Rappahannock River bottom fishing. (Courtesy of Danny and Mary Loving.)

Over the generations, most deadrise boats were built under God's sky. Later, builders built boat shops for building the boat inside. When built outside, a good-size tree was usually nearby to store lumber or to use the limbs to support a block and tackle for flipping the bottom of the boat over to start on the top work. (Courtesy of Joe Conboy.)

It should not be understated as to how much deadrise boats were used for transportation. When roads were poor, which was throughout most of the time, the main highways were the rivers and waterways of the bay. The boat *Frances* has an awning over the open part of the boat to keep passengers out of the elements. Deadrise launches were used to carry people back and forth to and from steamboats. (Author's collection.)

Beverley Ann is a classic round-stern deadrise boat. She has a unique little pilothouse. The boat was worked in the Rappahannock River crab and oyster fisheries and was in the same family for two generations. The family boat played an important part in the economic life of Tidewater Virginia and Maryland families. The photograph was taken in the 1960s. (Courtesy of Joe Conboy.)

Some 20 years later, the *Beverley Ann* was still owned by the same family and working on the same waters. She is seen here working in the summertime crab-pot fishery. If a wooden deadrise boat is properly maintained, it can be a generational investment for a waterman's family. (Author's collection.)

Lewis Wright of Deltaville, Virginia, built his first wooden boat as a boy in 1916. When this photograph was taken of him in the 1980s, Wright was building deadrise and flat-bottom skiffs at his boat shop on Lovers Lane in Deltaville. His boat shop is gone today, replaced by a summer home, but many folks up and down the bay have fond memories of having owned a Lewis Wright–built stiff. (Author's collection.)

Backyard boatbuilding was a cottage industry throughout the Chesapeake Bay region. This kitten found a comfortable perch on the stern deck of this round-stern boat that was being built in a backyard in the 1940s on Howard Street in Urbanna, Virginia. When a family needed a wooden boat, they knew where the boatbuilder lived to go get one built. (Courtesy of Wanda Greenwood Hollberg.)

Dr. A.L. VanName Jr. was the author's family doctor for most of his life. The two shared a love of maritime history, and Doctor VanName shared photographs that he had taken as a boy. This photograph is of his dog Jack in the wooden skiff he had as a boy growing up on York River. On the day this photograph was taken, Jack and "Van," as the doctor was called as a boy, were trotlining for hard crabs. The barrel held the baited trotline, and the hand dip net was used to catch the crabs. The Brownie camera case can be seen on the seat. Generationally, in Tidewater Virginia and Maryland, young boys had a skiff and a dog, which often resulted in priceless lifelong memories. (Courtesy of the Dr. A.L. VanName Jr. Collection, Deltaville Maritime Museum.)

BIBLIOGRAPHY

Chowning, Larry S. *Barcat Skipper: Tales of a Tangier Island Waterman.* Centreville, MD: Tidewater Publishing, 1983.

———. *Chesapeake Bay Buyboat.* Centreville, MD: Tidewater Publishing, 2003.

———. *Deadrise and Cross-planked.* Centreville, MD: Tidewater Publishing, 2007.

Dodd, Richard, J. and Pete Lesher. *A Heritage in Wood.* St. Michaels, MD: Tiller Publishing, 1992.

——— and Robert J. Hurry. *Boats for Work, Boats for Pleasure, The Last Era of Wooden Boatbuilding in Southern Maryland.* Solomons, MD: Calvert Marine Museum, 2009.

Gregory, Joseph E. *Deadrise is from here –To Yonder.* Yorktown, VA: Skipjack Publishing, 1987.

Johnson, Paula J., *The Workboats of Smith Island.* Baltimore and London: the John Hopkins University Press, 1997.

———. *Working the Water: The Commercial Fisheries of Maryland's Patuxent Rivers.* Charlottesville, VA: the University Press of Virginia, 1988.

Rabi, S.S. "The Art of The Bay Deadrise." *Maine Coast Fishermen.* April 1958.

DISCOVER THOUSANDS OF LOCAL HISTORY BOOKS FEATURING MILLIONS OF VINTAGE IMAGES

Arcadia Publishing, the leading local history publisher in the United States, is committed to making history accessible and meaningful through publishing books that celebrate and preserve the heritage of America's people and places.

Find more books like this at
www.arcadiapublishing.com

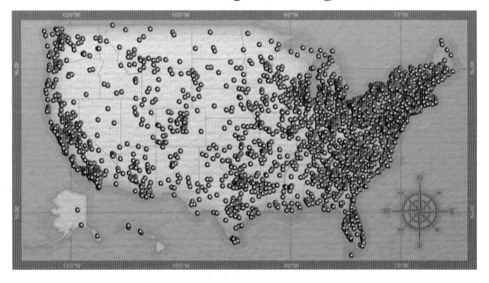

Search for your hometown history, your old stomping grounds, and even your favorite sports team.